371-425

ES

WORKING WITH

REAL LIFE GUIDES

Practical guides for practical people

In this increasingly sophisticated world the need for manually skilled people to build our homes, cut our hair, fix our boilers, and make our cars go is greater than ever. As things progress, so the level of training and competence required of our skilled manual workers increases.

In this new series of career guides from Trotman, we look in detail at what it takes to train for, get into, and be successful at a wide spectrum of practical careers. The *Real Life Guides* aim to inform and inspire young people and adults alike by providing comprehensive yet hard-hitting and often blunt information about what it takes to succeed in these careers.

Other titles in the series are:

Real Life Guide: The Armed Forces
Real Life Guide: The Beauty Industry
Real Life Guide: Carpentry & Cabinet-Making
Real Life Guide: Catering
Real Life Guide: Construction
Real Life Guide: Electrician
Real Life Guide: Hairdressing
Real Life Guide: The Motor Industry
Real Life Guide: Plumbing
Real Life Guide: The Police Force
Real Life Guide: Retailing
Real Life Guide: Working Outdoors
Real Life Guide: Working with Animals and Wildlife

trotman

Real Life

GUIDES

WORKING WITH YOUNG PEOPLE

Ian Pearson and
Dee Pilgrim

Real Life Guide to Working with Young People
This first edition published in 2006 by Trotman and Company Ltd
2 The Green, Richmond, Surrey TW9 1PL

Editorial and Publishing Team
Authors Ian Pearson and Dee Pilgrim
Editorial Mina Patria, Editorial Director; Rachel Lockhart,
Commissioning Editor; Catherine Travers, Managing Editor;
Ian Turner, Editorial Assistant
Production Ken Ruskin, Head of Manufacturing and
Logistics; James Rudge, Production Artworker
Sales and Marketing Suzanne Johnson, Marketing
Manager
Advertising Tom Lee, Commercial Director

Designed by XAB

British Library Cataloguing in Publication Data
A catalogue record for this book is available from the British
Library

ISBN 1 84455 054 0

Typeset by Photoprint, Torquay
Printed and bound in Great Britain by Cromwell Press,
Trowbridge, Wiltshire

Real
Life

CONTENTS

About the authors

Ian Pearson was Chief Executive Officer of the Institute of Career Guidance until October 2004 when he set up his own educational consultancy.

He holds a first degree from Exeter University and a postgraduate qualification from Westminster College, Oxford. Following a period in the Royal Air Force, he became a teacher and college principal. He has run a number of professional associations and has advised government departments on a range of educational and career issues. He has worked in the arts and complementary medicine and has been a teacher, examiner, tour guide and garden designer. He has written for *Young People Now* and *Newscheck* magazines, and contributed to the published Royal Society of Arts project on Professionalism in the Twenty-First Century.

Dee Pilgrim is a trained journalist who has worked as both a staff writer and a freelance for a variety of women's magazines including *Company*, *Cosmopolitan*, *New Woman*, *Ms London* and *Girl About Town*, and also for music publications. She is currently the film critic for *Now* magazine and is an active member of the Critics' Circle. She has written a number of titles for Trotman Publishing including Real Life Guides to *Carpentry & Cabinet-Making*, *Catering*, *Hairdressing*, *The Police Force* and *Retailing*, and *Performing Arts Uncovered*.

Acknowledgements

The authors would like to thank all the people who helped make this book possible by providing data and information, including Girl Guiding UK, the Scout Association and the Duke of Edinburgh's Award scheme. Special thanks go to those who took the time and trouble to talk about their own experiences of working with young people – Charlotte Adams, Jo Amand, Christine Dopson, Jeanne Hunter, Gail Jones, Lindsey Ledger, Nicola Martin and Tony Swan. A very special thanks to Phil Beadle, an inspiration to us all.

Introduction

Working with young people can be very rewarding, but it can also be very difficult and frustrating. It's not just about looking after nursery-aged children or playing football with your pupils, important though these activities are. It's also about dealing with a range of issues many people never experience for themselves. For example, you could be working with children with learning disabilities or who have been excluded from school for violent or disruptive behaviour. You could be working late at night on city streets with young people who have been the victims of abuse, or those who have problems with drugs or alcohol.

At times, working with young people will make you feel like a doctor, a nurse, a police officer, a social worker and a teacher all rolled into one.

Dealing with issues like these can be tough and it takes a special sort of person with a variety of skills to handle them sympathetically and successfully. It's about understanding others' needs and not imposing your own solutions. It's about being non-judgemental, yet offering support in ways that help others help themselves. It's about being firm but fair, and most importantly it's about having the ability to really listen. At times, working with young people will make you feel like a doctor, a nurse, a police officer, a social worker and a teacher all rolled into one.

So why, if it's such a difficult task, do so many people choose to do it? For most people who work with young people the answer is that they really feel they are making a difference. There's no better sense of achievement than knowing that your help and expertise has turned someone else's life around; that from a future that looked bleak and hopeless you have helped someone find hope and a brighter outlook. Seeing the difference your support and care can make can give a wonderful sense of fulfilment.

Despite some low salaries and, perhaps, a sometimes unglamorous image, most people who work in this sector love their work – otherwise they would never be able to deal with the constant demands it makes of them. They are dedicated to helping others achieve whatever is important to them. They respect each young person's unique skills, experiences and personality, helping them develop both as individuals and as people who can contribute to society as a whole. The reason this is so important is because the younger generation really is the future. The children and teenagers of today will grow up to become our doctors, lawyers, teachers, nurses, politicians and police, so society needs them to be well-balanced individuals who can achieve their full potential.

Seeing the difference your support and care can make can give a wonderful sense of fulfilment.

You may find it surprising just how many different jobs there are in this sector or connected with it. You could be working as a nanny with very young children, or you could be a social worker assisting troubled teenagers. You could be a teacher or even a police constable working as a Safer Schools Officer. The two charts below will give you some indication of just what you can do in this sector. The first shows jobs related to working with the under-fives, and the second shows jobs related to working with people over the age of five.

FIGURE 1: JOBS IN THE PRE-SCHOOL (UNDER-FIVES) SECTOR

NANNY →	FULL-TIME LIVE-IN PART-TIME LIVE-OUT
CHILDMINDER →	(ONE OR MORE CHILDREN; VARYING HOURS)
PLAYGROUP →	(ATTACHED TO CHURCH OR COMMUNITY CENTRE) SUPERVISOR MANAGER ASSISTANT
CRÈCHE →	(WORK-RUN OR PRIVATE) MANAGER ASSISTANT
NURSERY →	MANAGER NURSE ASSISTANT
DROP-IN CENTRE →	PROFESSIONAL VOLUNTEER
RELATED JOBS →	PAEDIATRIC NURSE MIDWIFE HEALTH VISITOR HOSPITAL PLAY SPECIALIST

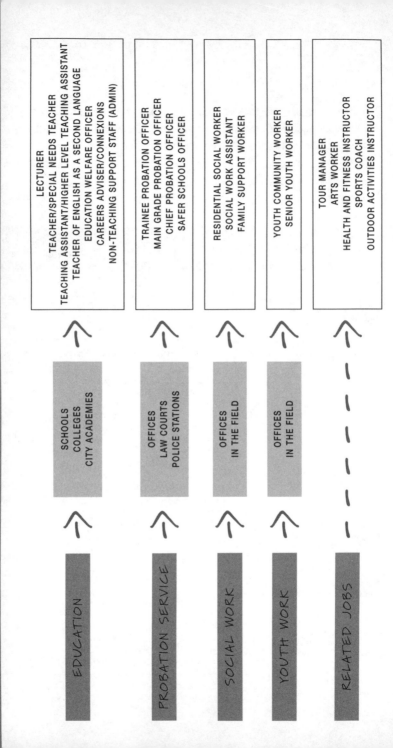

FIGURE 2: JOBS WORKING WITH YOUNG PEOPLE

EDUCATION → SCHOOLS / COLLEGES / CITY ACADEMIES → LECTURER / TEACHER/SPECIAL NEEDS TEACHER / TEACHING ASSISTANT/HIGHER LEVEL TEACHING ASSISTANT / TEACHER OF ENGLISH AS A SECOND LANGUAGE / EDUCATION WELFARE OFFICER / CAREERS ADVISER/CONNEXIONS / NON-TEACHING SUPPORT STAFF (ADMIN)

PROBATION SERVICE → OFFICES / LAW COURTS / POLICE STATIONS → TRAINEE PROBATION OFFICER / MAIN GRADE PROBATION OFFICER / CHIEF PROBATION OFFICER / SAFER SCHOOLS OFFICER

SOCIAL WORK → OFFICES / IN THE FIELD → RESIDENTIAL SOCIAL WORKER / SOCIAL WORK ASSISTANT / FAMILY SUPPORT WORKER

YOUTH WORK → OFFICES / IN THE FIELD → YOUTH COMMUNITY WORKER / SENIOR YOUTH WORKER

RELATED JOBS → TOUR MANAGER / ARTS WORKER / HEALTH AND FITNESS INSTRUCTOR / SPORTS COACH / OUTDOOR ACTIVITIES INSTRUCTOR

Jobs range from those needing few educational qualifications (such as childminder) to those requiring years of higher education (teacher or child psychologist, for example). This book focuses on those jobs that do *not* require full degree-based professional training: other books published by Trotman such as *Teaching Uncovered* by Brin Best and *The Directory of Teacher Training Courses* cover careers requiring degree or postgraduate qualification in greater depth.

In 2003 it was estimated that 2.4 million people undertook paid work with children and young people (under 18 years of age) and almost 1.8 million acted as unpaid workers or volunteers. However, the sector in general finds it hard to recruit the right people with the relevant experience and qualifications. The aim of this book is to help you decide if you are one of these 'right' people. It will identify the qualities that can help you get on and also the weaknesses that could hold you back. It will describe the positive aspects of the jobs, and it will also outline their downsides, giving you an honest overview of the sector. Not everyone is suited to working with young people but reading this book will help you decide whether you have the skills and talents it takes to succeed.

DID YOU KNOW?

In 2003, 11,000 local authority workers and nearly 40,000 youth workers outside local government employment were involved in youth care.

PHIL BEADLE

Success story

THE ADVANCED SKILLS TEACHER

Forty-year-old Phil Beadle is an Advanced Skills Teacher at a school in London's East End. However, he is probably better known to the public as the inspirational teacher in Channel Four's series The Unteachables. *In the programme a group of pupils who had attendance and behavioural problems was given the chance to participate in a special learning programme. Phil was immediately noticeable for his teaching style, including lessons such as 'Dickhead' and 'Punctuation Kung Fu'. Phil studied English and Drama at college. He has a PGCE, a BA Honours degree, two A levels and nine O levels. He has won awards for his teaching.*

'When I was at college I believed that being a teacher was politically the most useful thing that you could possibly do with your life,' *says Phil.* 'I always intended to be a teacher, but I thought it would be a good idea to get some life experience outside of the cloisters of lowbrow academia. Consequently, I spent my early adulthood acquiring this experience and didn't enter the profession until the age

Teaching is creative profession – you start with a blank page and a sea of new faces. By the end of the year th pages are fu and you knov the people behind the faces.

of 32. The biggest part of my job is teaching. I teach English and act as a model for the other professionals in the school. I observe other people's lessons, giving feedback, and I mentor a cohort of staff, helping to improve their practice. I also produce a newsletter about teaching techniques and write a column for the *Education Guardian*. Sometimes I go on telly talking nonsense too!'

Phil is obviously very successful at what he does and he believes this success is down to a variety of personal qualities. 'You need the ability to take risks and you also need self-belief,' *he explains.* 'You must have a sense of fun and a deep love of and empathy with children. Teaching is a creative profession – you start with a blank page and a sea of new faces. By the end of the year the pages are full and you know the people behind the faces.'

One of the most profound beauties of being a teacher is that – often accidentally – you will do at least one thing every day that makes a child's life better.

Although he loves his job, Phil is aware that teaching can be utterly exhausting, both physically and mentally. However, he would not change what he does. 'I am happy as I am and I am where I want to be. I have no desire to become a headteacher. I enjoy the respect I get from other teachers for remaining that: a teacher.'

The best piece of advice Phil can give anyone who wishes to follow him into teaching is not to let it take over your life.

'Don't take the decision to be a teacher lightly,' *he advises.*
'It is an extremely difficult career. It asks for more of you than
you would think were possible but, in doing so, it also offers
rewards that may well be greater than those offered by any
other job. As the American historian Henry Adams said, "A
teacher affects eternity. He can never tell where his influence
stops." One of the most profound beauties of being a
teacher is that – often accidentally – you will do at least one
thing every day that makes a child's life better.'

What's the story?

OVERVIEW OF THE SECTOR

In 2001 there were nearly 12 million children (those aged under 16) living in the UK. In Britain we have an ageing population (by 2014 there will be more people aged over 65 than under 16) because people are now choosing to have far fewer children than they did at the turn of the twentieth century and in general people are starting families later in life. However, the need for people to work with children and young people has never been greater. Experts seem to disagree on why children, especially those at risk, are in more need than ever, though some feel that changing patterns of family life, stress, the pace of life and the expectations of young people all play a part.

Young people's services are generally structured on a local authority basis. The overriding aim is always to deliver the right services as and where they are required – but beyond this, variations in delivery, between authorities or even within areas of an authority that have different needs, are common. Much of the current service was reviewed during 2005 and was affected by the Children's White Paper (originated in

The need for people to work with children and young people has never been greater.

2004), the restructuring of the 14–19 education curriculum, and some aspects of the 2005 Skills White Paper. These changes may affect the numbers being employed in this sector and the work they undertake.

Voluntary services also play an important and increasing role in the delivery of services to young people. The standards of service and the qualifications required by voluntary organisations are just as stringent as those of local authorities. And whether you specialise in working with the very young or with teenagers, you will have to undergo strict regulation, training and assessment. In fact, for most jobs where you will be dealing with children you will have to undergo a Criminal Records Bureau (CRB) check. More information on CRB checks is given in the boxes on the next page and on page 55.

An estimated £40 billion is spent annually on services to children, and about £61 million a week is spent by social services departments on children in need. In 1999–2000 voluntary organisations spent £367 million on delivering social protection services to children, while charities working in this area have experienced the highest growth rates in spending of all types of charities.

Whatever the overall context in which you will be working, young people need help, and you may be the right person to provide it.

THE CRIMINAL RECORDS BUREAU (CRB)

The role of the CRB is to 'reduce the risk of abuse by ensuring that those who are unsuitable are not able to work with children and vulnerable adults' (David Blunkett). In terms of working with young people, this means that if you have regular, unsupervised access to children you will in all likelihood have to undergo a CRB check – because you are in a position of trust and there is a need to see your full criminal history in order to assess whether you are suitable to carry out work of this nature. For more information, see www.crb.gov.uk.

TRAINING

There are many routes into training for work involving young people. Recent changes in education and training practice have made a wide range of options available, from those at National Qualifications Framework (NQF) Level 2 through Foundation and Honours degrees to postgraduate degrees and full professional training. Most training involves both practical and academic learning, so although aptitude is very important, so is the ability to study. For example, the Open University recently launched its Certificate course in Working with Young People, which assumes that you will be working in paid or voluntary work during the course and can draw on that experience.

The most common level of qualification within the sector is NQF Level 3 (some entry-level work is assessed as Level 2). However, attitude and personality are vital for success at all levels. More detailed information on the qualifications you will

DID YOU KNOW?

The National Qualifications Framework (or NQF for short) provides a way of comparing the relative levels different qualifications, in order to help you identify a clear progression route to your chosen career. All qualifications, once they have been accredited by the regulatory authorities, are included in the NQF. For more information and to view the current NQF, see www.qca.org.uk.

need is given with the job descriptions in Chapters 4 and 6.

CAREER DEVELOPMENT

If you want to progress in your career, most organisations encourage employees to continue their education and training. This could involve specialising in a particular area of work such as substance abuse, or being trained in management, or in business skills if you want to run your own establishment. Increasingly, organisations are looking for diploma and degree qualifications, or the potential for the candidate to commit to and successfully complete such training.

PERSONAL QUALITIES

Not only do you have to be able to relate to children and young people, you also need to communicate with a wide range of other professionals who are involved in the work. A professional attitude and a positive approach to understanding a common language must be accompanied by flexibility. Practitioners cannot be judgemental about the young people they work with, for whom a small 'improvement' may represent an enormous effort. One of the challenges of the work is to contribute not only a sympathetic ear but also a positive and informed attitude that presents more than a single resolution to any issue.

It is also important that practitioners see themselves as one of a team of helpers working with their young clients. The team may consist of parents, carers, local authority representatives and members of the legal, medical and social welfare systems.

Many people move into the sector from other professions such as teaching and nursing, and maturity is seen as a help in understanding the issues. Equally, young people wanting to work with others of a similar age are also encouraged to apply. Though they may be inexperienced generally, they can offer a real empathy and ability to understand the challenges facing young people trying to cope in the modern world.

It is also important that practitioners see themselves as one of a team of helpers working with their young clients.

In most cases, people working in this sector must undergo police background checks with the CRB (see pages 11 and 55) and receive training in child protection. Some organisations also ask for or provide first aid and other additional training.

EXPERIENCE

Past learning and experience are especially important in this sector, and all those entering training should ask about possible credit for prior learning. If you've already decided you want a career working with young people, one of the best things you can do to enhance your employment chances is to get some experience by volunteering.

VOLUNTEERING

There are many volunteer schemes across the country but details of three well-established organisations are given in the paragraphs below.

To be a volunteer leader in the **Girl Guides** you have to be part of its Senior Section. You can become a member of the Senior Section at 14 and you can remain a Senior Section member until your 26th birthday. A Young Leader is a member of the Senior Section who is aged 14–18 and no longer participates as a Guide. As a Young Leader you may choose to assist with a Rainbow (ages 5 to 7), Brownie (ages 7 to 10) or Guide (ages 10 to 14) unit.

With the **Scouts** you can volunteer in a similar way by joining its Young Leaders scheme. As with the Girl Guides, Young Leaders are aged between 14 and 18 years of age; they are Explorer Scouts who work with one of the younger Scout sections (such as Beaver Scouts or Cub Scouts).

The Young Leaders scheme allows participants to develop and grow as individuals, to make a valuable contribution to their community and to give service to others. You should find a welcoming, supportive atmosphere with plenty of opportunities for fun activities. The number of hours you give up will depend on which section you are working with and on your

DID YOU KNOW?

Over 42,000 students volunteered through organised programmes at their higher education institutions in 2004. Over half of all student volunteers are involved in projects involving children and young people.

Source: Student Volunteering England Research, 2004

other commitments. If you are aged 16 or over, you may work towards the Adult Leadership Qualification. There are currently 5453 Young Leaders in total, made up of 3831 males and 1622 females. If you are 16 or above you will have to supply two character references and also undertake a CRB check (see boxes on pages 11 and 55). At the age of 18, Young Leaders can become Unit Leaders. There are currently 70,000 Unit Leaders supported by 30,000 Unit Helpers and occasional helpers.

For more information see the Scout Association website, www.scouts.org.uk, and the Girl Guiding website, www.girlguiding.org.uk.

DID YOU KNOW?

Over 137,000 young people take up the challenge of the Duke of Edinburgh's Award every year with around 225,000 participating at any one time.

Source: www.theaward.org

Volunteering with the Girl Guides or the Scouts can help you to attain the **Duke of Edinburgh's Award**. Since it began in 1956, over 3 million young people have entered the programme and almost 2 million Awards have been achieved. You can also take part through schools, colleges, youth clubs, voluntary organisations (such as the Cadet Forces), pupil referral units, young offenders institutions and businesses. Most people are familiar with its 'Bronze', 'Silver' and 'Gold' award structure, each stage involving the successful completion of four components (service, skills, physical recreation and expedition).

However, there are also other parts of the programme, and one that is particularly relevant to those wishing to gain

experience working with young people is the Millennium
Volunteers programme. The Duke of Edinburgh's Award MVs
(Millennium Volunteers) are 16- to 25-year-olds who give up
their time for the benefit of others. They often get involved in
the leadership of their Award groups and gain a nationally
accredited MV award that demonstrates their commitment
to communities whilst developing skills such as leadership
and communication. MV is widely recognised by universities
and employers as providing an extra edge in today's highly
competitive environment. Activities like teaching others, peer
mentoring or helping within youth groups can all count
towards MV Awards. To find out more, see
www.theaward.org.

Tools of the trade

3

Most of the careers connected with working with young people do not entail what you'd call the usual Monday to Friday nine-to-five. Just think about it for a moment ... If you are working with young children in a nursery then you could be working half days, perhaps very early mornings when children are dropped off by parents or carers* on their way to work, or afternoons, or into the evenings as you wait for parents to return from work to collect their offspring. Many live-in nannies are on call from when the children get up in the morning until they go to bed, while teachers not only work during school hours but also have to do marking in the evenings and at weekends (and if they are interested in sports or other extra-curricular areas such as music or drama, they may well be supervising football, rugby or netball practice or directing rehearsals in their own time). A lot of full-time youth and community work involves evening and weekend work, while social workers and parole officers are often on call overnight and therefore work on a rota system. You could also be splitting your work hours between various different locations, depending on what you actually do.

All this means that working with young people is never going to be an ordinary job, and you need a lot of specific skills

*Note: Throughout this book, we use the term 'parents' to indicate either parents or guardians/carers as necessary.

and qualities to succeed. For a start you need to be flexible and to be able to think on your feet, but there are plenty of other character traits that will help you get on in this sector. By the same token there are weaknesses that could really hold you back. Below we list some of the emotional, physical and mental 'tools' you will need to give that extra boost to your career prospects.

PATIENCE
They say that patience is a virtue – and it is one that you will need in abundance no matter what age group of children you are working with. When a four-year-old wants you to sing *The Wheels on the Bus* for the twentieth time, you can't suddenly snap at them, or if a 15-year-old is having trouble telling you about a problem, you need to be able to let them do it in their own time. Have a good think about your levels of patience and be honest with yourself – do you tend to fly off the handle or simply walk away if you can't be bothered? If so, you don't have the patience to work in this sector.

MATURITY
When it comes to working with young people, someone has to be the grown-up, and if you are in a position of authority then that person is you. If you do not have a good degree of maturity, this sector could get the better of you. Being mature means you can keep a cool head and make sensible decisions in a crisis – which could be anything from a toddler being sick in playgroup to a teenager exhibiting threatening behaviour.

When it comes to working with young people, someone has to be the grown-up.

One of the best ways to become more mature is to get some experience, so think about volunteering with the age group you believe you are interested in eventually working with (see the volunteering section in the previous chapter for some ideas on how to get involved).

GOOD COMMUNICATION SKILLS

Talking to a three-year-old may well be very different from talking to a 13-year-old, but if you can't make yourself understood in either case, you are going to have difficulties working with young people. You will be talking to a wide variety of people every day – fellow professionals, parents and of course the young people themselves – and they will all need you to explain things clearly and efficiently. Communication skills work both ways, so you will also need to be able to listen to them and comprehend what they are talking about. Be clear, be concise and be firm in what you say. A definite 'yes' or 'no' is much better than a woolly 'maybe'.

GOOD SOCIAL SKILLS

You may find it difficult to get on in this sector if you are a bit of a loner or if you are not good in social situations. As mentioned above, you will be meeting a large number of people every day from all parts of society and they need to feel confident that you are more than capable of doing your job. You will need to be polite and to have a welcoming manner, no matter who you are meeting and whatever the situation. The young people you will be working with need to know they can trust you and rely on you, so if you smile and are friendly you will find it easier to put them at their ease.

PERSONAL DISCIPLINE

Young people are vulnerable and they rely on those who are there to help them, so you cannot let them down. Personal discipline is all about organising your own life and your own diary so you are able to keep up with your commitments. This ranges from good timekeeping to sorting out such things as marking or doing paperwork and keeping everything in good order. Remember, you are the person in authority, so the onus is on you to take charge and be in control. This will not happen if you have chaotic working methods, so get yourself sorted.

A SENSE OF HUMOUR AND PERSPECTIVE

If you can keep smiling while everyone else is having a sense of humour meltdown you will soon become a valued member of your working team. It is also a great way to relieve stress so, although you should never underestimate the difficulties of the people you are working with, an ability to see the lighter side is a great personal characteristic to have (especially when young Sally has just thrown yoghurt in your hair for the third time). When you are dealing with young people with real problems it is sometimes difficult to distance yourself from those problems, but you have to keep a sense of perspective.

TEAMWORK

People who work in this sector do not operate in isolation: most young people have a whole network of professionals, voluntary workers and family around them, and if you want to get on you must learn to fit in with this 'team'. You are all working in a co-ordinated fashion to achieve the best results and if there is good team spirit it will not only make the task go more smoothly but also make it a happier one. Your communication and social skills really come into play here, because no one wants misunderstandings, petty rivalries or office politics to take precedence over your real task, which is to improve the quality of young people's lives.

STAMINA

From dealing with a hyperactive five-year-old to a frenetic teenager with Attention Deficit Disorder, this is a career area in which you will really need all your energy and staying power. As stated at the beginning of this chapter, many jobs within the sector are not standard nine-to-fives in which you will be sitting behind a desk all day. In almost all cases you will be up and down, walking around, interacting with a lot of different people and constantly on the go. This is particularly true if you work in the pre-school (under-fives) bracket where you will spend much of your time chasing after children, picking them up, putting them down and sorting out play equipment. It can be truly exhausting so you need to be fit and healthy. If you take care of yourself you should be able to cope with whatever the little monsters can throw at you!

SELF-CONFIDENCE

Like animals, children have an uncanny ability to smell fear or indecision – and the minute they get a whiff of it from you, your authority will disappear out of the window. However, if you appear self-confident and in control it seems to breed confidence in others and it tends to make the people you come into contact with more willing to trust you and follow your advice or instructions. In many of the jobs we will describe in the following two chapters, the training involves confidence-building activities but, once again, getting some experience by taking on a Saturday position or some holiday or voluntary work can also be a big help.

If you appear self-confident and in control it seems to breed confidence in others.

While all of the above are positive attributes to think about when considering a career working with young people, there are obviously some personal characteristics that could hold you back. There are downsides and challenges to many jobs and it's good to know about them before you decide whether the sector is really what you want to do, rather than have to face them once you've already entered a job.

STRESS

Children are never predictable – that's what makes working with them such a joy: they are full of surprises. However, not knowing what they are going to get up to next can be the cause of anxiety and stress for some people. Having to constantly think on your feet and face new challenges can prove too much. Some jobs are also more stressful than others in terms of workload. For teachers, worrying about the class you have to teach tomorrow while fretting over the marking you have to do tonight can cause sleepless nights. If, despite your best efforts, a child appears to be failing, the pressure to help them succeed can seem enormous.

There are strategies you can follow to minimise stress (for example, exercise, taking up a hobby or relaxation therapies such as yoga or meditation) but if you would prefer someone else to be in control and you like a quieter life then you could consider one of the less stressful jobs available in this sector.

SHYNESS/TIMIDITY

If you can't think of anything worse than having daily face-to-face contact with a bunch of strangers, or if the thought of standing in front of a group of children and giving them instructions makes you tremble at the knees, then this really isn't the sector for you. Troubled teenagers can show hostility, the terrible twos can scream, shout (and sometimes kick), and even the most well-adjusted young people may sometimes need to talk in private to you about something that is bothering them. If all these scenarios make you shudder you may find positions that involve less personal contact, such as in the secretarial or administration areas, suit you better.

LONG HOURS

You've already learned that most jobs in this sector are not nine-to-five. Many involve long hours and some will also require you to work unsociable hours in the evenings and at weekends. If the thought of giving up time other people use for socialising doesn't sit well with you, then once again you should focus your research on those jobs within the sector that offer more structured working hours.

BACK PROBLEMS

Jobs in the pre-school (under-fives) area will be of most concern to those who have a family history of back problems. Picking up, carrying and putting down children can be back-breaking work. You'd be surprised how heavy a toddler feels by the end of the day – and that's before you add in crouching down to get in the Wendy House, lifting toys and bending over pre-school-sized tables and desks. If you know you are predisposed to problems with your back then it might be sensible to focus your research on another area of this sector.

Quiz

If you like the idea of working with young people but you are still unsure about exactly what you want to do, just try completing the fun quiz below. After each statement tick the 'yes' or the 'no' box and, when you've finished, take a look at the 'Answers' section to get some ideas on which area of employment might suit you best.

1 I wouldn't mind having to change nappies or clear up baby sick.

YES ☐
NO ☐

2 Large groups of teenagers really intimidate me.

YES ☐
NO ☐

3 I want a job where I always work in one place.

YES ☐
NO ☐

4 I want a job where I can really be hands-on and get stuck in.

YES ☐
NO ☐

5 I want a job that's really academic.

YES ☐
NO ☐

6 I want a job where the hours aren't too long.

YES ☐
NO ☐

7 I want a job that gives me a real sense of achievement because I know I have helped others to reach their full potential.

YES ☐
NO ☐

ANSWERS

1. If you answered '**yes**' and don't mind close contact with babies, and all that it entails, then working in the pre-school sector could be for you. If you answered '**no**', you might consider working with older children.

2. We read about teenage 'yobs' being served with ASBOs (Anti-Social Behaviour Orders) nearly every day in the newspapers, so if you answered 'yes' and you do feel intimidated, then be reassured – you are certainly not alone. You could work in the pre-school sector so that you are not exposed to this age group; or, if you do want to work with teenagers, a job that does not bring you into such close proximity with teenagers or means you meet them on a one-to-one basis may be more suitable – perhaps an administration position. On the other hand, if you answered '**yes**' and you do have the confidence to approach groups of teenagers and not feel intimidated, you might find you are well-suited to jobs such as youth worker.

3. If you answered '**yes**' you probably enjoy a sense of security in your surroundings, so a job where you go to the same crèche, nursery or school every day will give you a sense of familiarity. However, if you answered '**no**' and prefer to move around a bit more, a career as a student tour manager, travelling arts worker, field social worker or a parole officer might be of interest to you.

4. There is plenty of opportunity to get really stuck in, so if you answered '**yes**' you could think about jobs like outdoor activities instructor, sports coach or hospital play specialist, or you could try working in a playgroup or a nursery where you'll spend many hours reading stories, chasing toddlers around the floor and, you guessed it, singing *The Wheels on the Bus* again and again. If you answered '**no**', a more academic career may suit you (see next question).

5. If you answered '**yes**' you have probably already developed a love for learning, and by taking a job in academia – whether as a teacher, teaching assistant or special needs teacher – you will get the added satisfaction of seeing others learn. If you answered '**no**' and are less academically minded, don't worry – there are plenty of other jobs within the sector, from youth worker to family support worker, in which you can use your other skills.

6. A '**yes**' answer here may indicate that you don't want to work full-time. Well, don't worry: almost every job category in this sector employs part-time workers. This is especially true in the pre-school and youth community work sectors where you may only be needed for a few hours a day or even a few hours a week. If you would like to work in this sector while also holding down another job then why not consider

volunteering for a few hours a week?
There is a broad range of full-time jobs
available for those who answered '**no**'.

7 If you answered '**no**', this book is really
not for you. Working with young people is
all about helping them fulfil their potential
and in doing so getting a real feeling of
personal achievement. If you answered
'**yes**', congratulations! You've got what it
takes to make a real success of this
career.

By now you should have a better idea of
what you will need to help you get on in
this challenging work arena. If you've got
what it takes, Chapters 4 and 6 will explain
exactly what it is you can do in the sector,
first with the pre-school age group, and
second with those who are aged five years
or over.

DID YOU KNOW?

One in ten children and young people aged between 5 and 16 had a clinically recognisable mental disorder in 2004.

Source: Mental Health of Children and Adolescents in Great Britain Report 2005

4

Pre-school – working with the under-fives

Provision of services for the under-fives varies throughout the UK. The current government has developed the 'Sure Start' programme to upgrade early years provision. Its aim is to deliver the best start in life for every child in England* by bringing together early education, childcare, health and family support and by offering supportive training to those who wish to work in the sector.

In general, this sector is not well-paid and it relies on the commitment of thoughtful and caring people. In fact, volunteers working under the supervision of trained professional staff carry out much of the work. Although there are many excellent employers who treat their staff well, there is a high staff turnover with many people choosing to move to more lucrative work. However, if you are strongly committed to working with small children, or you want the experience, challenge and responsibility of doing so, then the opportunities are many and varied and job satisfaction is high. You may be a great influence on a child's life, helping them to develop early skills.

*Responsibility for early education in Scotland, Wales and Northern Ireland rests with the separate devolved administrations.

Early years is an area of work in which experience really does count, but many employers also look for qualifications (such as an NVQ in Early Years Practice or a Certificate in Work with Children) to complement and formalise experiential learning. The Sure Start website (see Chapter 9, Resources) lists a large number of courses leading to qualifications in the early years sector that qualify the holder for a listing under their Childcare Approval Scheme. The scheme includes many mainstream qualifications and some specialist courses leading to work, for example with Montessori schools. There are many agencies working in this area which can find either full- or part-time work for prospective employees.

You may be a great influence on a child's life, helping them to develop early skills.

One thing you should be aware of if you plan to enter this sector is the bias towards female workers. This has come about because, traditionally, it has always been women who have been responsible for child-rearing. As more and more women have gone back to work after having their children, their preference has been to leave them in the care of other women who are possibly mothers themselves. Attitudes towards men caring for young children are proving quite difficult to change – many people are still wary about male nannies or male nursery workers. If you are a male wishing to work in this sector you should take on board that most – if not all – of your co-workers will be female and that some people may still view your choice of career with mistrust. However, there is no reason whatsoever why men shouldn't do these jobs – indeed, in London, male nannies have become quite fashionable, especially if their charges are boys, because it is thought they can be good male role models.

This chapter will explore the types of job available working with the pre-school age group, giving an indication of the type of work, the skills you might need, the pay, the working conditions and the qualifications required.

CRÈCHES

Crèches are designed to care for small children during working hours while their parents are otherwise committed. Some are run within company workplaces and shopping centres, while others cater for the local community. A single, committed (and paid) individual helped by volunteers is a common model of this type of organisation. Company crèche schemes are often offered as part of a work package and provided for employees either free or at minimum cost.

Consider carefully the prospect of working with other people's children all day and then welcoming home your own in the evening!

The work is varied and may include organising play, feeding, changing and generally caring for small children who may be with you for an hour or two or for the whole working day. Much of the work is part-time and may suit those who have small children of their own and can work during school hours. However, if you are in this position, consider carefully the prospect of working with other people's children all day and then welcoming home your own in the evening!

Most schemes run by local authorities – and many others – ask for NVQ qualifications from potential staff, though some will take on an unqualified person if they agree to undergo training within a specified timeframe. Most commonly, you will need NVQ Level 2 or a BTEC National Award. As many workers are only part-time they get paid an hourly rate of between £5 and £12 depending on experience and training.

NURSERIES

Nurseries fill the need for childcare when the parents are unable to look after their children themselves. This may be during working hours, but it could also include evenings and weekends. The distinction between a nursery and a crèche is blurred, but in general nurseries are more likely to be attached to schools and to fall under the OFSTED inspection system, and are less likely to be found in shopping centres and within company workplaces.

Some nurseries operate only during the day and on a small scale, while others offer extensive hours and additional services such as child collection, employing highly qualified nursery staff and managers. There are casual and part-time posts available as nursery assistants and nursery 'workers' – these posts are often advertised locally and may be filled by staff who do not have formal training in the area.

DID YOU KNOW?

Ofsted is the inspectorate for children and learners in England. Their job is to help improve education and care by carrying out inspections on nurseries, childminders, schools, colleges, teacher training providers, local authorities and other organisations. For more information, see www.ofsted.gov.uk.

Many nurseries are either located on school premises or have specific links to schools in the area, feeding into primary school 'foundation' years. All nurseries may be inspected and those linked to the formal education system are subject to inspection by the Ofsted team (see box). All members of staff have to undergo a CRB check (see pages 11 and 55) and to undergo child protection training.

Working in a nursery can be extremely rewarding, as many of the children will be there for several hours, several days each week. They therefore become well-known to the staff. The children learn social and community skills and frequently form friendships that outlast the nursery. In addition to caring for the children, nursery nurses may undertake other work such as promotional activities, teaching and administration. Many are encouraged to undertake further training and to develop skills for business and management.

The children learn social and community skills and frequently form friendships that outlast the nursery.

It is worth being aware that nurseries vary in quality – some are excellent, professionally organised outfits with well-qualified, well-managed staff and excellent facilities, but others are under-resourced, often with unmotivated, poorly managed staff, poor facilities and worn-out equipment. Toy hire and libraries do exist in some areas to help nurseries keep up to date, though even a few beans in a tin may provide hours of fun and learning. All nurseries may be inspected and those linked to the formal education system are subject to inspection by the formal Ofsted team.

Nursery work is an area where experience is as valuable as formal qualifications but most full-time nursery workers must either be qualified or be working towards qualification. Most employers ask for at least an NVQ Level 2 for entry into the profession though some will accept those willing to undertake such training. Senior nurses and managers are expected to hold at least NVQ Level 3 qualifications. There are now also Foundation degrees in nursery work. All courses involve some practical work within nurseries. In order to work with children unsupervised you will need a Council for Awards in Children's Care and Education (CACHE) Diploma in Child Care and Education, or NVQ Level 3 in Early Years Care and Education.

In some cases, teachers or nurses qualified in the care of adults may retrain to take senior posts in nursery care. There are few opportunities for those aged under 16 and all people working in the area are subject to police background checks with the CRB (see pages 11 and 55). Starting salaries are around £8000 to £10,600 per annum. Those in senior posts can earn between £17,400 and £23,400 and these positions may attract pension and other benefits.

NANNYING

Nannies work with private individuals, usually caring for young children of pre-school age. Conditions and work vary considerably depending on the ages and needs of the children concerned and the expectations of the parents.

A diverse and trained workforce has replaced the traditional image of nannies walking large prams in the local park and meeting with other nannies of a similar 'cultural' background. Though there are no formal qualifications for the role, most parents and all professional agencies will require their nannies to have undertaken some form of childcare training.

The skills required for the work will vary, but an ability to work with children, care for small children's needs and teach older children basic social and learning skills may be necessary. Some children are taught at home and the work of the nanny may be extended to or supplemented by that of a home-based tutor.

Autonomy and the ability to organise your own working day are also seen as added incentives to undertake the work.

There are qualifications available in early years childcare, and experience may be gained through voluntary work. There are BTEC First Diplomas (NQF Level 2) in Caring and in Early Years, while CACHE offers a Foundation Certificate in Caring for Children. Some mature students may see formal training as a way of using their own experience of caring for children or they may already have suitable training in a related area (such as teaching or nursing) that could be useful.

Being a nanny is not a nine-to-five job and hours can be long with little financial compensation. Some see the opportunity of living with and enjoying the facilities of the family home as adequate compensation for the hours worked. Autonomy and the ability to organise your own working day are also seen as added incentives to undertake the work.

How much you earn will depend on your hours of employment, how many children you are looking after, your qualifications and experience and also where you are working (nannies working in London should expect London weighting, ie extra pay to offset the cost of living in the capital). For example, recent advertisements in *The Lady* magazine for live-in nannies included one for a nanny in Putney in London to look after a one-year-old girl and a two-year-old boy for £400 per week, and another for a nanny in Oxford to look after a girl of five and boys of two and seven for £300 per week. Some agencies offer work overseas, so nannies with language qualifications are particularly sought-after and can command significant salaries.

The National Childminding Association has just started to offer membership to nannies and this can help to demonstrate that you have a professional outlook. Check the website at www.ncma.org.uk. It would also be helpful to undertake the government's voluntary Childcare Approval Scheme (see page 37).

SUPERNANNY

Jo Frost is the 34-year-old star of the hit TV series *Supernanny*. Jo has always had a gift for connecting with kids on their own level, and began babysitting as a teenager. After college she embarked on nannying as a career and now has 15 years' experience as a nanny in England, the Caribbean and the United States. Her experience and knowledge mean she is able to give parents practical and objective advice that goes beyond the normal boundaries of being a nanny. The advice she gives is based on a relationship with the parents as well as the child, developing an environment of honesty, openness and trust.

Jo has been so successful that the original TV series is now being aired in 47 countries and there is also an American version of the series. Jo has written a book on parenting, also entitled *Supernanny*, which has been translated into a number of languages including Japanese and Hebrew, and she has set up her own business, B4UGo-Ga-Ga, where parents can approach her and her team for hands-on help with child-rearing problems. As if that weren't enough, Jo currently writes a monthly column in *Practical Parenting* and has a weekly column in the *Sun* newspaper.

CHILDMINDING

Childminders work in their own homes looking after a number of children of varying ages. Whilst most of the work is with the under-fives, some minders will cater specifically for older children. Many childminders work part-time, though some work long hours providing early morning, late night and weekend services to parents.

Childminders must be able to deal with a wide range of children's demands, from physical and mental needs to basic education and play. They must be highly organised and capable of working closely with parents and teachers as well as the children in their care.

While no formal qualifications are required, childminders have to register and they and their homes are inspected regularly to ensure they meet the current national standards. All minders (and family members over 16) and their staff are required to undergo checks with the CRB (see pages 11 and 55). The National Childminding Association (www.ncma.org.uk) now has 50,000 members. It promotes and provides information on the sector, and aims to support those working within it by organising training courses.

Childminders should get at least £7000 a year, but those with better qualifications and especially good reputations can earn £25,000. Childminding is a business and most minders are self-employed, so career enhancement opportunities are rare. Some childminders specialise in working with particularly demanding children and some practitioners go on to qualify in related areas of child and healthcare.

THE CHILDCARE APPROVAL SCHEME

This is a voluntary scheme for approving childcare providers and enabling parents and employers to check whether a carer is approved. It is run for the Department for Education and Skills (DfES) through the Sure Start unit (see start of chapter) and came into effect on 6 April 2005. The scheme provides recognised national status for individuals providing childcare in the child's own home or, for children aged over seven, on other domestic premises.

The scheme:

- Verifies that the individual has a suitable childcare qualification
- Verifies that the applicant has undergone appropriate first aid training within the three years prior to the date of application
- Carries out an enhanced CRB check including a POCA (Protection of Children's Act) list check. (For more information on CRB checks, see pages 11 and 55). The Childcare Approval Body will then assess whether the CRB disclosure or entries on the POCA list contain information that would make the applicant unsuitable to work with children.

The scheme is voluntary and applies only to childcare provided in England. Approval is valid for one year and as the scheme is self-financing a fee of £96 is payable, which includes the cost of the CRB check plus VAT.

A national helpline is available during business hours on 0845 767 8111. Calls are charged at the local rate or higher rate from a mobile or public phone. More information is available on the website www.surestart.gov.uk/childcareapproval.

Source: Sure Start

PLAYGROUPS

Playgroups are often (though not necessarily) located on school premises and may constitute part of a primary school's organisation. As such they are subject to local authority regulation and Ofsted inspection. Alternatively they may be controlled by other organisations, such as churches or charities, and there are also a few commercial companies operating in this area.

Work at a playgroup may consist of story reading, drama activity, sports, music and other activities carried out in a safe and supervised environment. Playworkers should be aware of the health and safety aspects of their work as they often work unsupervised, sometimes in unusual locations such as adventure playgrounds, and they may be required to carry out site visits.

Playgroups may operate in term time only and staff may be involved in the education of the children as well as in their general care. In this setting, play is seen as an educational activity, and knowledge of the values of play and the underpinning methodologies of how young people learn is invaluable. Alternatively playgroups may operate in the early morning as a pre-school club, after school hours or throughout holiday periods as 'holiday clubs'. Some authorities have supported schemes that enable play leaders

Play is seen as an educational activity, and knowledge of the values of play and the underpinning methodologies of how young people learn is invaluable.

to visit many different sites or to travel in a 'play bus' visiting rural areas in particular.

Supervisors of playgroups are qualified to at least NVQ Level 3 or NNEB Diploma (National Nursery Examining Board) standard and are often qualified teachers. A team may consist of a manager, supervisor and assistants, so a form of career path is available to those who are interested in promotion. Some staff may be engaged without qualifications if they have agreed to study for those qualifications, normally in pre-school work or childcare.

Due to a number of government initiatives, this sector is currently expanding rapidly, and there are good opportunities for promotion, so getting as many qualifications as possible – such as HNC or HND (Level 4) – makes good sense. There are also many specialised courses such as the BTEC Diploma in Specialised Play for Sick Children and Young People. Salaries start at around £10,000 but as you gain more experience you can expect to earn up to £23,700.

DROP-IN AND HOME VISIT CENTRES

Some communities, voluntary sector companies and religious groups organise drop-in centres where children can play and where their parents can speak with professionals in childcare. Some

DID YOU KNOW?

According to government figures, in 2002 in the UK there were:

- 152,016 nursery nurses
- 113,437 childminders and people in related occupations
- 61,825 playgroup leaders and assistants.

Source: 2002 Census

organisations also arrange home visits, when they are requested, for parents who are experiencing specific challenges or who have asked for specific forms of support.

Working in this area requires an understanding of children, their carers and the environments in which children are brought up. See also Hospital Play Specialist on page 67.

5

Case studies: pre-school

CHRISTINE DOPSON – NURSERY ASSISTANT

When Christine Dopson decided to go into childcare she was looking for a different kind of reward. After many years of working in caring professions and having taken NVQ Level 4 qualifications in Social Work, she still felt dissatisfied. As she was unqualified in nursery work, Christine opted to work as a nursery assistant while she gained her qualifications. She chose to use an agency that arranged work for her and organised courses that she undertook in her spare time.

'If I was asked to assess a person's suitability for this work, I would ask them to play with some children – if they get down on the floor to establish eye contact and play the children's games, they are going to make it. You can't do this job sitting in a chair,' *says Christine.*

A large part of a nursery assistant's work is playing with children in a constructive way. This may be using playdough, paints,

> You can't do this job sitting in a chair.

puzzles, paper, bicycles or pushchairs, but the play has to be thought through and constructed in such a way that children experience a range of activities and social experiences.

'Children learn to develop skills with their hands and in co-ordination, but they also have to negotiate, to understand that things don't belong to them but to the group,' *Christine explains.* 'It's an important step in understanding how to work in social groups and learning to share with others. Working on puzzles is the beginning of developing problem-solving skills, and singing and reading picks up on rhythms and sounds – and it all feeds the imagination.'

A typical day at Christine's nursery begins around 7.30am, with children being dropped off as their parents go to work. All children have a breakfast, either brought with them or provided by the nursery staff, and then go to the story area to have a story read. It is then outside playtime with bikes, pushchairs, the sand pit and other toys until elevenses (if it's wet, the children use the community room). There's more play until lunchtime and after lunch is rest period. Some children leave, others arrive and then in the afternoon the morning sequence is repeated until around six o'clock when the last parent collects their child.

The thing Christine likes the most about her job is working with others who are also committed to childcare, the children themselves and their openness, and the fun of playing. Christine admits to being lucky in that most of the nurseries she has worked for have been very professionally organised.

When you feel that small hand slip into yours, you know that not only have you been offered the child's trust, but you have also been put in a position to have a positive influence on that person's life.

Many nursery staff operate through the agency system, including young people starting out on their career and those wishing to work part-time. 'I would recommend the work to those starting out,' *Christine comments.* 'But you need to feel a real calling. It wouldn't have interested me when I was leaving school, but some of my friends went into nursery work and loved it. They trained at the local college and worked at the same time. And there is a career path too, if you want to manage or own your own nursery. Look at the local authority-run nurseries as well as privately operated schools and decide which suits you best. And remember, no one system is necessarily better as all nurseries have their own distinct style. It's down to the people involved.'

Christine loves what she does and certainly knows all about job satisfaction. 'When you feel that small hand slip into yours, you know that not only have you been offered the child's trust, but you have also been put in a position to have a positive influence on that person's life. That's when you know you have made the right decision. Childcare is so rewarding.'

JEANNE HUNTER – NURSERY NURSE
Jeanne has been in nursery nursing for nearly 40 years. And she is still committed to the work and its benefits. Now a

day care co-ordinator in a city nursery, she welcomes the changes that have been made in the profession and even looks forward to the Ofsted visit. 'Inspection is good,' *she says;* 'it keeps us on our toes and makes sure we are up to date and the staff are well trained. We all benefit, especially the children, who are given an excellent start in life. Yes, the paperwork can be very time-consuming and it takes you away from the children, which is not a good thing, but overall things have greatly improved.'

Nurseries rely upon a good strong team of workers, many of whom may be part time. Jeanne has tried working in both commercial childcare and local-authority-supported work but much prefers the latter. 'You have more opportunities to train and to really develop a career,' *she says*.

'I would take young people on placement, but employing them can be more difficult. You do need some experience of life in general, but even so, good professional training is really necessary. It's not enough to be a caring and sympathetic child-lover,' *explains Jeanne.* 'You must understand how children learn and to have a range of techniques to help them. We used to have to make our own toys, or make a set of dolls' clothes – all sorts of practical things – but now it's much more complex. The children haven't changed much but the expectations of parents and the demands of the education system are much greater. You need full professional training.'

Jeanne has fought hard to have the qualities of nursery nursing recognised at national level. 'Nurses have so much to offer in themselves as well as in support of teachers and others working in the sector. Our training has improved so much that at last we are getting the recognition we deserve. I completed a course on Early Years Learning and found that I knew as much as the teachers.'

Every day is different — it's full of variety. I love working with the children and I love working with their parents too, offering them the reassurance of a safe and secure environment for their child.

'There are specific ratios of children to staff that are set nationally and must be adhered to. This can give rise to staffing problems in terms of ensuring cover at all times, and does add to costs. All nurseries are run on tight budgets. Good practitioners constantly review their practice in order to improve. Sometimes it may take days or weeks of concentrated effort to find that one contact point that opens up a child. They all have good in them; it just takes time. That's not box ticking or form filling – it's practical common sense and hard work.

'I can honestly say that I have really enjoyed my years in childcare. I have had good and bad times but overall it has been so worthwhile. There's too much paperwork but I would never change my career. Every day is different – it's full of variety. I love working with the children and I love working with their parents too, offering them the reassurance of a safe and secure environment for their child.'

TONY SWAN – CHILDMINDER

Tony Swan has always been interested in young people and how they work. During his first year at university he read Child Psychology as one of five subjects, before going on to get a BA Combined Honours in Economics and Law. He subsequently went to work in the city with computer systems but became involved in childcare when he and his wife, who was already a registered childminder, had young children of their own. He started off as an assistant but became a registered childminder to give himself more control of his working life. He is now responsible for a number of children (some with special needs) from as early as 7.30am until 6pm, and his duties include changing nappies, sorting out dietary requirements and supervising free play as well as leading constructive play. Although he now works nearly full-time he can still fit in enough leisure time to indulge in his passion – rugby coaching and building up a Mini and Youth Rugby section at Teddington Rugby Club.

'I love the freedom this job gives me to organise my own life,' *he says.* 'Also, the support and rapport you build up with the children and their families is wonderful. Watching the children's development and knowing you play an important part in their lives is incredibly fulfilling, and it's also a lot of fun.'

However, Tony does acknowledge that sometimes it can get to be a bit of a chore – especially nappy changing. There are also the times when children arrive feeling unwell, when they can be especially demanding. Because of this he says you need to be fairly laid back and relaxed with children in order to make a success of childminding. 'You need to enjoy their company – some people can't stand them! You need to be a leader, but you also need to be able to follow instructions: if a parent says they don't want their child to have milk, there may be a life-threatening reason for this.' *Tony also makes the interesting comment that* 'childcaring by yourself can be lonely, so you may find working with another childminder, in a nursery or respite care centre with companions your own age, is more fun.'

He thinks the best way to see if it is for you is to actually go out and do it. 'Suck it and see. Give yourself, say, six months, working in a nursery environment or with another childminder to make sure you enjoy what you are doing. This will also provide you with initial guidance in how to do the job.'

I love the freedom this job gives me to organise my own life. Also, the support and rapport you build up with the children and their families is wonderful.

Tony has no ambitions to take more NVQs or courses in order to go on to run his own nursery. He likes the freedom to control his own life that the present position affords him and he enjoys what he does enormously. 'It's really only when you start doing the job that you realise how important it is. Looking after other people's children cannot be done by a machine. Six months to three years is a very formative period of a child's life, and your involvement and contribution is far more than simply running a crèche so the parents can go to work. By spending the better part of the day with a child you become something of a role model and, after a while, almost a member of their family.'

6

Working with young people

Chapter 4 has already covered the pre-school age group, so this chapter will cover working with young people aged over five. There is an enormous variety of work available with this age group – as you have already read, in 2003 it was estimated that 2.4 million people undertook paid or voluntary work with young people. Broad areas include education, social work, legal services, youth and community work, health and fitness, and all sorts of other jobs such as student tour manager or arts worker. Each of these areas will be explored in more detail in this chapter, but before going any further, we need to lay down a basic definition of 'young people' – where does the age group start and finish?

HOW OLD ARE YOUNG PEOPLE?
Secondary education traditionally meant education from the age of 12 to the end of compulsory education, currently 16. However, now that nearly half of all students stay on to take advanced level qualifications, many pieces of legislation include students up to the age of 18 or in some cases 19. This creates a slightly confusing situation but, for the sake of argument, this chapter will cover activities for those aged under 19 but over five.

EDUCATION

TEACHER/FURTHER EDUCATION LECTURER

Most roles in education require specific, degree-based qualifications, and all school teachers need to hold Qualified Teacher Status (QTS). Further education (FE) colleges also teach the 16–19 age group, focusing on vocational training and the acquisition of practical skills in conjunction with academic training. For FE lecturers, professional training and experience may sometimes be acceptable in place of QTS, and you may also need to qualify as a National Vocational Qualification (NVQ) assessor.

Salaries for those who have QTS start at £18,558 in state schools but can rise to over £90,000 for a headteacher of a secondary school in London. As explained in the introduction, this book will not cover the profession of teaching in detail; more detail on this career area is available in *Teaching Uncovered* by Brin Best and *The Directory of Teacher Training Courses* (Trotman Publishing).

CLASSROOM ASSISTANT/LEARNING MENTOR

There are very few posts available for those who do not have or are not working toward QTS, though some LEAs (Local Education Authorities) and some independent schools may consider employing classroom assistants or learning mentors who are not holders of QTS. Classroom assistants are directly involved with the learning processes for students who require additional expertise or possibly language help. Learning mentors fill a different role, helping students through difficult periods and acting as a supportive adult.

TEACHING ASSISTANT

Teaching assistants (TAs) and the new category of higher level teaching assistants (HLTAs) help qualified teachers, who supervise their work. TAs and HLTAs may be qualified to undertake work within particular subject areas, curriculum areas or special needs requirements. They help students to achieve goals agreed between the teacher and student by:

- Providing additional teaching
- Developing special packages of work
- Using visual aids or specific learning support (for example, to help those with disabilities).

In the latter case this may involve using expertise in signing, Braille work or aiding the physically disabled with mobility issues. The work is largely term-time only and many posts are part-time. You have to be committed to teaching and, in the case of special needs, to have an understanding of the challenges involved and current thinking on their resolution.

Whilst maturity and experience are important prerequisites, many TAs have or are working towards formal training in a particular field. You have to be 18 to start training as a teaching assistant, taking NVQs to Levels 2 and 3 or CACHE Levels 2 and 3. There are a number of courses designed for those who are working with children with learning disabilities including hearing impairment (BTEC Award in Support for Deaf Learners – Level 3) and Braille. Part-time Foundation degrees for teaching assistants may be available in your area. Salaries start at £10,000 and can rise to £14,000.

If this work particularly appeals, you may be interested in other related forms of employment with charities and further education colleges or you could undertake in-service training to qualify for a speciality.

TEACHER OF ENGLISH AS A FOREIGN LANGUAGE

One area worth considering is teaching English as a foreign language (TEFL). This area of work usually involves teaching English language to students from countries other than the UK, offering additional tutoring on the language skills that are already taught in their own school or college system. Typically the work is seasonal and concentrated in a small number of language colleges, though there are opportunities for year-round work. Teachers qualify by passing at least a certificate-level course in language teaching (such as Trinity's TESOL qualification or Cambridge's CELTA) and are often previously qualified in teaching or another profession. Courses can be delivered on a one-to-one basis or in groups. TEFL is sometimes wrongly seen as a soft option: in fact it is highly skilled and demanding work in an increasingly competitive and commercially driven market sector.

Most language colleges and some other schools run summer courses for both overseas and UK-based students. Supervisors and skilled staff are recruited specifically for their expertise in dealing with young people. Senior members of staff usually need professional qualifications in teaching, counselling or specific skills (such as sailing or football coaching), but many posts are available to students and others who can show an aptitude. Salaries vary widely, but a teacher of EFL just starting out should expect to earn £12,000 per annum.

EDUCATION WELFARE OFFICER (EWO)

Education welfare officers act as the link between students, parents and the school or college authorities. They investigate issues such as attendance, and try to identify and resolve the problems behind such behaviour. This may include challenges with family life, health and child protection issues. EWOs may be involved in arranging education and learning for those excluded from school, helping families to apply for benefits and entitlements, and assessing pupils with special educational needs. Welfare officers need to have an understanding of the issues that confront both students and their carers. They may need to work closely with other professionals in Connexions, legal, health and social services (all covered later in this chapter).

Working patterns vary and may include significant amounts of evening and weekend work. EWOs may be based in schools or local authority offices, or they

DID YOU KNOW?

The Teaching Awards were set up in 1998 in order to promote teaching as a career. Every year all 29,000 schools across England, Wales, Scotland and Northern Ireland are invited to nominate outstanding headteachers, teachers and teaching assistants. In 2005 there were winners in 142 categories and ten national winners, including the BT Award for Teacher of the Year in a Primary School, the Award for Special Needs Teacher of the Year, and the Award for Teaching Assistant of the Year. The winners received their awards at a ceremony held at the Theatre Royal, Drury Lane, London in October, which was televised by the BBC.

Source: The Teaching Awards

may be based from home. The nature of the work demands a mature and experienced approach. You need to have a caring attitude and to be able effectively to implement the current legislation, which may include giving evidence in court and furthering the prosecution of parents.

Education welfare officers act as the link between students, parents and the school or college authorities.

Applicants for this work frequently come from other professions such as teaching and social welfare, but those with experience rather than academic qualifications may be considered. Working experience will often be supported by study for a social work or education welfare qualification. Career progression is possible through a local authority (or other employer) to obtain a management role or a senior professional post. Training in this area of work is currently undergoing change and you should check with your local education or social service authorities as to the current requirements. Starting salary is at least £14,817 a year but senior EWOs can earn £30,000.

All those working in this area are subject to checks with the CRB (see box opposite and page 11) and have to undergo child protection training.

THE CRIMINAL RECORDS BUREAU (CRB)

In the past some organisations could conduct checks on details held by the police and government departments to identify unsuitable prospective employees – but most could not. In particular, organisations engaging volunteers had very limited and inadequate access to such checks. In some cases information was known to the police which, had it been made available to employers, would have prevented offenders from being employed and being able to harm vulnerable people.

The Disclosure service implemented through the CRB has been designed so that relevant information can be made available to many more organisations – but always with the consent of the individual applicant. This enables these organisations to make safer and more informed recruitment decisions – which is particularly important for positions involving trust of any sort. Such trust is critical in posts involving contact with the vulnerable.

Under the previous system, the police forces of England and Wales had never been specifically resourced to carry out the checks required of them. Furthermore, the demand for these checks had been rising steadily. As a result, some forces were having difficulty in meeting the demand within agreed turnaround times. Extending the scope of the previous system would have placed an intolerable burden on the police. So the new system centred on the CRB was conceived. Under this new system the police are properly remunerated for the checking and information they provide. This ensures that they can fund and pursue their core crime prevention function more fully.

In addition to their civic concerns about the exploitation of the vulnerable, citizens have needs in their capacity as prospective employees or volunteer workers. In these roles they need to be reassured that the Disclosure service will ensure that they are evaluated fairly and that their rights to privacy are not prejudiced. The CRB has addressed this issue in a number of ways.

- No Disclosures can be issued without the consent of an individual applicant.
- The information provided on Disclosures is always provided to individual applicants. If they are unhappy about any aspect of it or believe it to be wrong they can challenge it and have it reviewed.
- There are increased safeguards in the Code of Practice to ensure that personal information provided by the CRB to any organisation remains confidential. This is to ensure that the individual's rights to privacy should not be abused.

In July 2005, the CRB issued its seven-millionth Disclosure.

Source: Taken (with permission) from the CRB website: www.crb.gov.uk.

NON-TEACHING SUPPORT STAFF

All teaching establishments employ a number of non-teaching support staff. These may be caretakers, playground supervisors, technicians, resource specialists and librarians, and administrative and reception staff. All staff, including those on part-time and short-term contracts, may be subject to police background checks with the CRB (see previous box and page 11) and child protection training. Indeed some local authorities are now implementing training courses for all their support staff that may include work on inclusion, special needs, risk assessment, child protection and safety.

Conditions of work vary, and if you are interested in working in schools and colleges as a support staff member you should contact your local authority. In the case of a private school you may wish to contact the school directly. There are a number of national and local agencies that provide support staff and undertake personnel screening on behalf of the employers.

SOCIAL WORK

FIELD SOCIAL WORKER

Field social workers work within the community, often in a team with other professionals. They offer help, advice, practical assistance, counselling and protection to vulnerable people. The work has been described as rewarding but 'frustrating and emotionally challenging'.

> **DID YOU KNOW?**
>
> Britain has at least 175,000 school-age children with caring responsibilities for family members. One in five of them has educational difficulties or misses school.
>
> Source: Young Carers in the UK Report, 2004

Much of the work involves challenges facing children, young people and those who care for them. This may include dealing with families or individual children who are at risk, in care, or in foster or adoptive homes. Field social workers are also involved in trying to maintain family units that may be under pressure owing to some form of abuse or legal procedure. The work requires you to provide practical advice and guidance, go through formal procedures and also offer a sympathetic understanding of the challenges of family life. Workers must be able to gain the confidence of the people they are dealing with and their professional advisers. They must display patience, care and understanding while maintaining a professional stance. Social workers encounter a wide range of lifestyles, personal preferences and abilities. They must remain non-judgemental and open-minded and they need to have a strong knowledge of relevant areas of the law and legal procedures. They must be thorough in their record keeping and be able to manage a significant and demanding caseload.

Workers must be able to gain the confidence of the people they are dealing with and their professional advisers.

They may work with local authorities, charities, the prison service or commercial organisations. Because of the nature of the work, hours are irregular and often include weekend and evening working, so flexibility and mobility are essential.

Qualified social workers must hold a degree in social work approved by the General Social Care Council and must be registered with that council. Entry to courses is by the usual academic routes and may include working on an access or other preliminary course. Voluntary work, prior learning and experience are all important and may be taken into account by universities. Both full- and part-time courses are available for initial learning and many courses are available for those already working in the field but who want to progress to Master's level or to specialise. For holders of a first degree that is unrelated to social work it may be possible to qualify by completing a social work diploma or a Master's level course.

There are agencies that help social workers gain employment. They can expect to earn a starting salary of between £15,000 and £22,000 (depending on qualifications and experience) while senior social workers earn upwards of £28,000.

RESIDENTIAL SOCIAL WORKER
Some social workers are employed in care or children's homes, hostels and other centres. They work closely with other professionals to provide support, advice and learning to vulnerable residents who may suffer from a range of illnesses, disabilities or difficult circumstances. They help to create a safe environment for young people and their families by assessing individual needs and offering support. As part of this work they may accompany residents on outside visits and holidays.

Residential social workers need to be very patient but firm in the support they offer. Some of the work may involve court actions and they must therefore remain professionally objective and maintain accurate records. Full-time qualified social workers have to be registered, but some part-time posts for unqualified or partially qualified workers may be available. Shift work is common, as is evening and weekend working. There are opportunities for voluntary work, which may be used as a route into full-time working and qualification.

Local authorities, charities and private providers all employ residential social workers. Agencies exist to manage self-employed social workers. The sector is frequently understaffed and the demand for qualified social workers is high.

DID YOU KNOW?

In 2002 there were 78,379 social workers employed in the UK.

Source: 2002 Census

SOCIAL WORK ASSISTANT (SWA)

As the name suggests, social work assistants help qualified social workers with their workloads by undertaking visits, assessing needs, contributing to teams and following up on appointments and meetings. The work is often practical, varied and demanding and may be organised on a shift system or by an 'on-call' arrangement. It may take place in a number of settings including the home, hostels, hospitals and the community.

Training is often undertaken on the job and may lead to Level 2 or 3 qualifications. Many workers commit to a Foundation degree or other higher-level qualification. Previous experience, especially of working with children and young people, is an advantage. Applicants must be over 18 and have a good general education. Some of the work may lead to legal actions so workers must be professional about record keeping and meticulous in their dealings with the clients. A flexible approach, an open attitude and location mobility are essentials.

FAMILY SUPPORT WORKER
Trained and experienced workers, often from a social work, childcare or teaching background, carry out family support work. The work involves visiting families in their homes and offering support, information and advice to those undergoing particular stresses.

It may also involve court appearances, so as well as a caring and understanding attitude, family support workers have to be knowledgeable on the law, meticulous in their record keeping and extremely professional in their approach. Support workers may be called upon at any time, so a positive attitude to flexible working is required. The job may involve working with other professionals as part of a team of specialists.

Support workers ... must be non-judgemental, supportive, understanding, informed and well organised.

Support workers need to be expert communicators and team workers, with an informed approach to childcare, learning and development as well as expertise in running a home. They must be non-judgemental, supportive, understanding, informed and well organised.

Currently, training for this area of work is often based on childcare or social work qualifications. On-the-job training is possible for those who do not have relevant qualifications but who do have significant work experience of young people and families. Whilst most work is within local authority structures, some large charities also employ workers in this field. Salaries are in line with those of social workers.

PROBATION SERVICE

PROBATION OFFICER

Probation officers work with offenders, and sometimes with the victims of criminal activity. They do not work with young people exclusively, but much of the work does involve young offenders. The work is varied and may include preparing reports, supervising and enforcing sentences and assessing offenders for release. Working with the victims of criminal activity may include visiting homes, advising them on available professional help and helping the rehabilitation processes.

The working week may include late nights and weekend shifts. Some roles involve extensive travelling. Probation officers need a mature and non-judgemental approach and strong communication skills. They also need to be able to write concise and cohesive reports, to appear in court, to manage time effectively and to prioritise.

All those working in this sector are subject to police background checks with the CRB (see pages 11 and 55) and have to undergo child protection training. If you

DID YOU KNOW?

There were 10,964 probation officers working in the UK in 2002.

Source: Office of National Statistics

join the Probation Service as a trainee, you are able to study for the Diploma in Probation Studies, which is the prerequisite for working as a qualified Probation Officer. Entrance at trainee level is assessed on a mixture of experience and academic qualifications. There are special access opportunities for mature candidates. Voluntary or part-time work within a social work or vulnerable persons setting is particularly relevant. Check with your local probation service for the current requirements. Salaries start at around £13,000 a year for trainees, while main grade probation officers earn between £19,000 and £26,000. Chief probation officers can earn in excess of £32,000.

DID YOU KNOW?

268,480 offences were committed by children and young people aged 10 to 17 in 2002-2003.

Source: Youth Justice Board Annual Review 2002-2003

If you are interested in careers with the Police Force, for example as a Safer Schools Officer, more information is available in the *Real Life Guide to the Police Force* (Trotman Publishing, 2005).

YOUTH AND COMMUNITY WORK

Although policy is set at national level, in practice each county organises its own service to suit the specific needs of the communities it serves. This is a logical arrangement, but it does give rise to large disparities between employment opportunities in different areas – so the first thing to say is that if you want to work in the youth and community sector you *must* check with your local authority before assuming either that local roles exist (with vacancies) or that the levels of training required are at least equal to the national standards.

Typically a county structure may consist of a Youth Service, caring for young people between the ages of 13 and 19, a Youth Offending Team (part of the Youth Justice Service) caring for those aged 10–17, and a wide-ranging voluntary sector. A county Youth Service may be divided into geographically sited teams operating from neighbourhood centres or clubs as well as having a central presence in a county headquarters. The teams may offer services such as counselling, mentoring and advice on social inclusion, and contribute their expertise to joint projects set up within their specific areas. Others who work closely with the Youth Service include Connexions personal assistants and educational welfare workers.

In addition to the local authorities, much youth and community work is carried out by the voluntary sector, including religious organisations and national and local charities. Most of the larger charities have terms and conditions of service, quality, training and qualification requirements to match, if not exceed, national standards. However, some smaller local charities may accept volunteers with fewer qualifications, and these may provide positions for gaining work experience. Almost all charities rely on a large team of volunteers, and many employers would be looking for voluntary experience as a significant factor when assessing a job candidate's suitability and commitment.

THE NATIONAL YOUTH AGENCY
Founded in 1991, the National Youth Agency is funded mainly by the Local Government Association and aims to support those working with young people.

- It influences the shaping of youth policy.
- It aims to improve youth services.
- It promotes young people's participation, influence and place in society.
- It provides a unique national resource for practitioners who work directly with young people.
- It publishes a wide range of books, magazines, posters and games.
- It helps secure standards of education and training for youth work.

To find out more check out the website at www.nya.org.uk.

YOUTH AND COMMUNITY WORKER

Youth and community workers provide informal guidance, advice and help to young people. They may work from a base in the local school, college, community centre or youth club. Some operate as outreach or detached workers, meeting young people in places where they congregate – for example clubs, bars, cafes and even on the street. Youth workers are closely linked to the government Connexions service, which is discussed more fully later in this book.

Youth workers help young people who are experiencing challenges such as difficulty at home, health issues, or drug or substance abuse. They also aim to pre-empt or prevent some of these issues by working on community projects, and by counselling and informal advice and guidance. Some work through performance, helping to put on plays, music and other work.

Some youth and community workers may also be involved in dealing with young offenders and may be part of a Youth Offending Team. Youth workers invariably need to work with other professionals such as social workers, teachers, the police and the probation service.

Youth workers help young people who are experiencing challenges such as difficulty at home, health issues, or drug or substance abuse.

Many youth worker positions are part-time (or voluntary) and will probably involve some unsociable hours including weekend and night work. It's very important to be available when you are needed because much of the work relies upon building a relationship of trust between the youth worker and the young people. You must be able to understand, or at least empathise with, the varied needs and demands of young people, some of whom may be outside what are generally regarded as the social norms. You should have a keen interest in the things that most young people enjoy, from music and fashion to sport and the latest technologies. You must have organisational skills, patience and stamina. You will be subject to police background checks with the CRB (see pages 11 and 55) and will have to study the current child protection regulations.

Most full-time youth workers are professionally qualified through a degree or diploma course validated by the National Youth Agency. Part-time or voluntary workers may not be so highly qualified (there are qualifications at NVQ

Levels 2 and 3), but they often feel the need to understand their profession more fully and choose to study part-time to obtain recognised qualifications at a higher level. Many youth workers are mature adults who are either changing careers or bringing relevant experience into the profession.

As with other areas of socially orientated work, the pay and conditions of service are not good, though the rewards in terms of job satisfaction are very high. For those with good qualifications the starting salary is around £14,000, while senior workers earn around £28,000. Opportunities do exist for career progression in local authorities and large charitable organisations.

OTHER ROLES

HOSPITAL PLAY SPECIALIST

This is demanding but very satisfying work, dealing with children from all age groups who have been admitted to hospital (or other medical centre), or who may be ill at home. The work may include working in paediatric departments, accident and emergency units, hospices, or in the community. Hospital play specialists help children to adjust to and understand the new environment and their particular condition. By using informed play techniques, they enable the patients to express their thoughts and concerns whilst having fun. Their role is essentially creative and enabling, using art, music and drama to create a safe and trusting atmosphere in which the children can explore their new

> **DID YOU KNOW?**
>
> According to government records there were 79,498 people working as youth and community workers in 2002.
>
> Source: 2002 Census

surroundings and react to their changing condition, which may involve illness, surgery or other medical procedures.

Work of this nature requires flexibility in terms of hours worked and the conditions under which work may have to be carried out. Patients may need help at any time and on any day. Those considering this option for work should think through the implications for their own home and social life. The rewards are gained from the satisfaction of seeing the responses of the patients and their carers. Attempting to understand and meet the needs of the individual child is demanding and requires a high level of professional skill and experience. Equally, parents and other carers who may be worried, distressed or themselves suffering from illness, disability or other problems will need to be treated with patience, understanding and practical assistance.

Hospital play specialists help children to adjust to and understand the new environment and their particular condition.

It is possible to work in this field without formal qualification (for example as a hospital play assistant), but if you want to work in the NHS as a qualified specialist you should obtain the Level 4 BTEC Professional Diploma in Specialised Play for Sick Children and Young People. All applicants for the diploma have to be over 20 years old and must have worked with children in a paid or voluntary capacity. A mature attitude is very important and many entrants have previous experience of childcare or teaching. Salaries start at £12,000 but senior play co-ordinators can earn £30,000.

CAREERS WORK AND THE CONNEXIONS SERVICE

Impartial and independent careers advice can help young people to focus their education on the future that most interests them. Well-trained careers advisers use their skills to challenge students' assumptions, assess their abilities and provide them with information on a range of options for further training, employment or personal development.

Impartial and independent careers advice can help young people to focus their education on the future that most interests them.

Careers advice is currently delivered to students via the Connexions Service and via careers co-ordinators within their own schools and colleges – this section will cover career opportunities in both these areas. Recent proposed changes to the curriculum may affect how careers advisers work in schools and colleges – for example, if the recent proposals to create a greater mix of vocational and academic opportunities are implemented, then careers work will become even more important to students and teachers.

The work is ideal for those who want to help young people resolve some of their problems. It is rewarding to know that you have been able to use your expertise to help others.

The Connexions Service aims to provide all those aged between 13 and 19 with a 'one-stop shop' offering expert advice on a wide range of issues. Although Connexions itself is currently undergoing some restructuring, the service it provides will continue to exist, even if the name is changed. **Connexions staff** come from a wide variety of backgrounds: some are teachers, others have had previous careers in social work, still others have experience of human resources (HR) work. They work in schools and colleges as well as in high street offices. These are sometimes located with the local authority youth service but remain independent of that service and any other government-sponsored agency.

Connexions staff can be drawn from a wide range of careers and early training. They must undertake courses to familiarise themselves with the Connexions procedures and range of services. The majority of the Connexions Service is delivered by private and competitive companies who offer training and promotion prospects. However, terms and conditions do vary throughout the UK and in some cases local authorities or their subsidiary companies undertake the work. Check with your local office and, when you respond to job adverts, make sure you understand the local structures. Salaries start at £18,000 rising to £35,000 for a middle manager.

Within schools and colleges some teachers and lecturers – not Connexions staff – also deliver careers information and guidance. **Careers co-ordinators** seek to bring together all the skills and expertise available both within the school or college and externally, especially for those about to take A levels or advanced NVQs. Whilst some careers teachers are specialists, many are not, teaching a wide variety of subjects and taking additional training to fulfil their careers role. Training for work may be taken through a variety of routes including NVQ Level 3 courses in Guidance or through appropriate degree-level work.

HEALTH AND FITNESS INDUSTRY

Do you like the idea of sharing an eight-hour shift in a windowless box with 20 other sweaty people accompanied by thumping urban music? Or perhaps you would prefer a tranquil scene in a luxury hotel with a swimming pool and mini-gym where wealthy people cheerfully pedal away the pounds? Or perhaps you can see yourself living aboard a Caribbean cruise liner, helping the pampered to keep fit in the sunshine? Welcome to the varied world of the health and fitness industry, currently enjoying a significant growth period.

Sports groups offer young people somewhere to meet and help them to develop good health habits.

This is reflected by the fact that young people are being catered for in increasing numbers. It is good business sense to encourage young members (who may stay with the club for several years) but, in addition, there is growing concern about the long-term consequences of poor fitness levels amongst young people. The social benefits of fitness are sometimes overlooked – but sports groups offer young people somewhere to meet and help them to develop good health habits. Regular exercise may become the groundwork from which professional athletes emerge, or simply contribute to sustained healthy living.

Training requirements and opportunities vary enormously. Some clubs require no formal qualifications, preferring to train people on the job, while there are posts for those holding degrees and postgraduate qualifications in such areas as nutrition and sports science.

You might also consider acting as sports coach to schools and colleges. Some, especially in the private sector, take on temporary or short-term coaches, and many summer schools offer sports and activity courses to students. Most educational centres ask for specific qualifications in coaching sports (not necessarily a teaching qualification), but check first – some organisations may offer entry-level work, which does not require specific awards. A trained Health and Fitness Instructor should earn about £11,000 when starting out but experienced instructors can earn £30,000.

TOUR COMPANIES

Educational and cultural tours are a major source of income for UK-based tour companies. Every year, thousands of students from the United States and other English-speaking countries (such as Canada) visit the UK to experience a new culture and to learn something of the European way of life. Many students (and their teachers and parents) have roots in the UK so they use their visit to look up relations and to explore counties and towns associated with their families. Typically a visit of at least three weeks would include parts of the Republic of Ireland, Scotland,

Wales, England (especially London) and possibly an additional trip to Paris, Rome or Barcelona.

You may be able to develop a reputation for excellence that is taken up by specialist companies.

Tour managers (sometimes called guides or directors) work on a self-employed basis to conduct these tours and to fulfil the itinerary requirements. The work is demanding and highly seasonal, extending for a few months in the summer (especially June and July) with very little available out of season. Experienced guides may find companies to work for throughout the year and if you can offer a particular expertise (for example a sport or interest such as photography) you may be able to develop a reputation for excellence that is taken up by specialist companies. Knowing the companies, their specialist key staff and how to access them is essential if you intend to build a career in this sector.

You need to have an interest in young people and their concerns, some knowledge of the history and culture of the areas to be visited, and infinite patience. As well as being responsible for organising the tour itinerary, managers are required to conduct walking tours around major cities and to offer information on the history and cultural significance of the towns and cities visited. A background in teaching or lecturing is therefore helpful (but not essential). Touring with up to 50 people who are all relying on you can be fun, but it is also tiring and demanding work. It helps if you have experience of independent travel in a wide variety of countries. That experience will give you a confident, assured attitude and will translate well into helping others who are travelling in a new environment and may be away from home for the first time.

Formal training for these posts is minimal and tour managers have to rely on their own experience of travel, their expertise in organising people and their ability to work well with a variety of other professions. Pay varies depending upon your expertise, experience and other factors, but it is usually based on a daily rate plus expenses. Most tour managers rely upon visitors' 'donations' to make the trips financially viable. For those who are employed all year round by a reputable firm, salaries can start at around £12,000, but with training and experience you can earn up to £25,000.

If you have language qualifications, it may be possible to work with a company that specialises in bringing foreign language students to the UK. As well as gaining cultural experience, these students will be practising their English and need help in doing so. Knowledge of French or Spanish is especially helpful, though other languages, such as Japanese, are also in demand.

ARTS WORKER

If you think you have a talent for performance you might consider working in an arts organisation that specialises in young people's performance work or the delivery of product to young people. That last phrase was deliberately chosen to give you an idea of what you might encounter. 'The Arts' are not just about creating things – they are also about selling and delivering quality 'product', on time and within budget. So if your expertise is in an area other than performance (for example administration, business skills or crafts such as costume making) you might explore the possibilities.

Outreach work, usually based in an arts centre or connected to a theatre company, often includes work with young people, either through the school or college system or through local clubs and voluntary organisations. It can be very rewarding work as well as an excellent way of improving your own performance skills.

In some areas funding has been made available to support theatre companies specifically designed to work with young people. They provide theatre performances and tour within their area. In addition they work closely with teachers, supporting their work, and arranging workshops or classes that explore curriculum books and themes.

It can be very rewarding work as well as an excellent way of improving your own performance skills.

There are a number of commercial companies that recruit performers to organise out-of-hours or weekend drama clubs for young people, sometimes on a franchise basis. These opportunities are as much about operating a business as they are about creativity, and must therefore be seen both as a performance opportunity and a business venture for a niche market.

All those working in the arts need to have drive and determination as well as talent. A large number of courses and training schools exist for most of the arts disciplines. Many courses are at degree level and all require evidence of practical aptitude for the art concerned. There are also a small number of training schemes and placements for positions such as arts administration or directing. Competition for places on these schemes is extremely fierce.

Many opportunities in the arts world, especially at entry level, attract little or no salary, but they attract plenty of applicants. Because entry is so competitive, be aware that many employers in the arts will want to see evidence that you can actually do the work as well as knowing the theory. Any work experience will help to convince employers that you are serious and committed to the sector.

The arts world does attract many people who believe the glamorous image that is sometimes promoted. The reality is very different: it requires disciplined hard work, stamina and commitment. There are few formal career patterns and most people work their way into jobs by using their own initiative and networking skills.

7

Case studies: young people

GAIL JONES – TEACHER

Gail is the Head of Department and teacher of ICT skills at a busy inner city school in Liverpool. She came to the education profession late, going to university in her early thirties to study for a degree and to take a teacher training course. She became more interested in what she was doing as she studied, especially after the two teaching placements that formed part of her training. She now teaches eight different classes varying in size from a Year 7 group of eight pupils (her most difficult group, for which she has a classroom assistant) to her top set Year 11 group of 29 pupils (there are only 29 computers in the classroom).

'What I like most about what I do is working with the kids, and the interaction and humour they provide. I especially like working with the pupils who are coming up to taking exams and helping them to achieve qualifications. It's also great working with the other staff because they

> What I like most about what I do is working with the kids, and the interaction and humour they provide.

are a real source of support and camaraderie – much needed when you are having a bad day! However, one of the downsides of the job is the fact that there is too much paperwork and it takes you away from teaching. There's not enough time to complete all the work you are set within a term without using your own leisure time. But the worst thing about the job is watching able kids choose to fail. This can be soul-destroying at times, especially when you and the team you work with have done everything imaginable to help them change track.'

Gail believes that in order to succeed you need to be both hard (so as not to take offence at the way the kids treat you) and soft (so that you can listen and understand when they are having a bad time). A good teacher will know when pupils are trying to play them between the two.

It's also great working with the other staff because they are a real source of support and camaraderie — much needed when you are having a bad day!

'I would like to stay as Head of Department, because the next step would be to become a member of the Senior Management Team and that would mean less time in the classroom and less time with my family,' *Gail explains*. 'I do want to progress to be a better teacher and I would like the time to try new teaching skills and more time to observe other teachers. This is especially true in the ICT area because it's hard to keep up with all the new innovations in software and hardware – it's a subject that never stands still.'

Gail gives the following advice to anyone who is thinking of becoming a teacher. 'Research the job properly by talking to other teachers and don't do it just for the money or the holidays.' *She also suggests finding out what financial support is available – for example, trainee teachers in certain 'shortage' subject areas are eligible for extra funding.*

CHARLOTTE ADAMS – TEACHING ASSISTANT

Charlotte always wanted to work with children but had never considered working with children with special needs. However, she got a job at the Greenmead School, Putney, for children with special needs, by doing work experience there when she left school. That was 12 years ago and Charlotte is still at Greenmead. She has done a two-year childcare course on a youth training scheme, giving her NVQ Level 1 and 2 qualifications. This enables her to carry out tasks such as feeding children who have had gastrostomies, replacing gastro tubes, administering rectal Valium (an emergency drug for epilepsy) and using suction machines for children with tracheotomies or who have poor swallowing control.

'I support the teacher in a classroom of six children and there are another three assistants working with me,' *says Charlotte.* 'The children are aged between three and 11 years and all have severe disabilities. During the course of a day we will work with computers, standing frames, physiotherapy groups and music groups. We have a sensory room and do a lot of sensory work, including swimming. The other assistants and I also provide a bus escort for the children.'

You need to be patient, understanding and willing to learn. You should be prepared to be pleasantly surprised.

Charlotte enjoys what she does so much she says she will never change her profession. She is always busy and says she learns something new every day. However, one of the occupational hazards of working with children with disabilities is all the lifting and hoisting it entails – this can lead to back pain and muscular strain. You need to be physically fit to do what Charlotte does. But this has not put her off – in fact she would like to progress by taking further qualifications in childcare (such as those offered at NVQ Levels 3 and 4) and to achieve her ultimate ambition of managing a caring agency or a respite centre for people with special needs.

Charlotte says that there are many personal skills you need if you are going to be successful at caring for people with disabilities. 'You need to be patient, understanding and willing to learn. You should be prepared to be pleasantly surprised because there is more to life than just a wheelchair. If you are seriously considering doing what I do you should visit a school or set up a work placement so you can prepare yourself. It will help you to decide if you feel up to the task.'

NICOLA MARTIN – COUNSELLOR
Nicola has always been interested in people and what makes them tick. After doing an Honours degree in Social

Science she worked as a locum social worker in a hospital, and that is when she became interested in working with cancer patients, especially teenage cancer patients. She then went on to do a postgraduate degree in Social Science (Social Work) and went back to work in the hospital where she had been a locum, training on the job and attending conferences and workshops. Two years ago she moved to work in a hospice that caters specifically for those who are terminally ill with cancer. The patients range in age from young children to elderly people but the majority are young adults.

'I provide counselling and support not only to the patients but also to their families. I work on what the impact of a deteriorating illness will mean to them. I work with children prior to their parent's death and also following it, giving them bereavement counselling. I also provide support for the other team members at the hospital but bereavement counselling is my biggest duty – working with art, modelling plaster, painting and colouring as a form of therapy. With the parents who are patients I help them before they die by collecting "memory storage" where we prepare photographs and mementoes for their children.'

You need to have a good balance between your work life and your private life in order to make this career a success.

For Nicola, working with the children is the best thing about her job, especially when, after a few sessions, she sees them start to pick up and express themselves through creative activities. She likes to see them get back on their feet. She also likes working with a close, supportive team. The downside of the job is that there is a lot of sadness attached to it. Nicola feels you need to have a good balance between your work life and your private life in order to make this career a success.

'You need to be able to recognise when you have had a bad day and go and do something about it. That's why it is essential to have a sense of humour to do this job. You also have to have the ability to connect with people, to be patient and to be a good listener. The best way to see if it is for you or not is to go and do some work in a care environment. Take a summer job in a residential home, do voluntary work with a children's summer camp or work at a youth club or local charity for a week – that will soon let you see whether you have got the commitment to do this job or not.'

LINDSEY LEDGER – YOUTH WORKER (VOLUNTARY SECTOR)

Greater freedom, flexibility and a chance to develop her own skills were among the reasons Lindsey Ledger decided to change her career direction and move from being deputy head of a primary school to being a youth worker in the voluntary sector. Volunteering to work with local youth and children's groups helped Lindsey through a severe illness, but once she had fully recovered she realised that she had found her niche. She is now a paid member of a Community Church Youth Organisation and manages 40 volunteers working on projects for children and young people aged from under two to 19.

'In a small voluntary organisation you don't have a party line,' *she says.* 'You do what is right for the circumstances you are in. It's great working with real people and real problems. It was time for me to change, and youth work uses my teaching skills in a practical and direct way. My work is based on Christian faith and values, but you don't have to be a Christian to do wonderful things. And those we help can come from any – or no – religious group.'

As a volunteer, you see people in a different context and they see you not as a 'manager' or a 'teacher' but as a helping hand.

'Youth work can frighten some people; they might feel intimidated by the images they see in the media. In practice, most young people are great to work with. In many ways volunteers are not valued by society, but they are really appreciated by those who benefit from their work. It can be frustrating to see so much need and not enough resources, and working with volunteers demands advanced communication skills. The typical volunteer does put people first, but is really focused on seeing the results: that's what really counts. And you relate to people in a different way – you are not a manager or a teacher. As a volunteer, you see people in a different context and they see you not as a "manager" or a "teacher" but as a helping hand.

'We employ several people on a part-time basis who can bring their skills to the team. We have trained community workers, teachers, specialists in volunteering, communications experts and those who are great at organising. We even have a life coach who runs courses for young people who need to think through their needs and expectations. We spend some time fundraising for projects such as holidays for deprived children, but most of our work is directly with the young people themselves. I think we offer not only fun, but also a structure and a discipline which most young people really appreciate.'

Lindsey uses her training as a teacher but has added to her range of skills by taking short courses and learning from other more experienced practitioners. 'We encourage all our staff to take regular training and to attend a wide range of meetings,' *she says,* 'and we offer a range of courses on specific subjects to increase their skills and confidence. We also encourage young people to take part and have a Young Leaders course aimed at 14- to 18-year-olds who want to learn more about youth work. They cannot take full responsibility for the work but they can develop skills and it may lead to them wanting to become fully qualified in the profession. Peer group leadership is really important in youth work.'

Youth work can frighten some people; they might feel intimidated by the images they see in the media. In practice, most young people are great to work with.

Starting as a volunteer, whatever your age, can give you a real insight into the work. Your time will be valuably spent and may include everything from helping the very young to read and write to taking football training and even to teaching management skills. You may work in an office, a youth centre or a church. You will certainly need organisational skills, good interpersonal skills and commitment, and if you are good at fundraising so much the better. Many small charities are prepared to consider training young people and taking on those who are not yet fully qualified but are working towards qualification.

JO AMAND – SENIOR YOUTH WORKER (LOCAL AUTHORITY)

Jo had no initial interest in working in this profession, but when she did the Duke of Edinburgh's Award, part of which entailed community service, she started working with people with special needs. From there, Jo branched out into working with youth clubs, play schemes and after-school clubs. After doing her A levels she left school to work part-time for the London Borough of Harrow and she took its in-house youth work qualification, accredited through the Open College Network. When she was 22 she took a postgraduate national qualification in Youth Work on a day-release basis at Brunel University. In September 2000 Jo started to work for Wandsworth Borough Council and now, at the age of 25, she is its senior youth worker. Ultimately Jo would like to progress into project development because she likes starting new things and watching them grow. For this she will need to build up her levels of experience.

Jo's current duties include supporting the tutoring staff and the careers advisers, doing a lot of work face to face with young people, and also having to cope with a lot of administration such as publicising the opportunities for young people in the borough.

'I started out co-ordinating the Duke of Edinburgh's Award scheme in the borough and my duties have progressed from there,' *she explains.* 'Now I don't work so much with youth clubs but with special projects such as dance and drama courses and web design courses for young people from ten to 19 years old. I also train teachers and other youth workers to get the qualification that will enable them to run outdoor trips. Another job I'm doing at the moment is organising a scheme over the summer months to supervise Year 11 pupils who are at risk of falling through the education net.'

You need to have a very open mind to do what I do. You really have to have a good understanding of where other people are coming from.

The diversity and challenging nature of the job are what Jo enjoys most, along with actually being able to see young people progress because of the advice and support she gives them. But one of the downsides is that she sometimes wants to help young people who don't want to accept her help. There are also a lot of guidelines and legal requirements she has to adhere to for her own safety and the safety of the people she works with, and this can be frustrating.

Jo is very specific about the personal attributes she feels she needs in order to do her job. 'You need to have a very open mind to do what I do. You really have to have a good understanding of where other people are coming from. You definitely need patience and to be able to use your intuition, and I would say it is very important to be consistent and to deal with people in a consistent manner.'

The last word

By now you should have a better understanding of what
working with young people entails and what jobs are actually
available. Working in this area can be fun, exciting and
personally very rewarding. It can also be intensely frustrating
and very challenging. However, if you believe you've really
got what it takes to succeed there is enormous scope for
career advancement, mainly through gaining more
experience and undertaking more training (such as going on
to Level 4 NVQs or doing a part-time degree course). There
is also the possibility of moving sideways within the area –
say, from being a nanny to studying to be a nursery nurse –
depending on your experience.

There are a number of things you can do while you're still at
school that can add to your levels of experience and give
you a helping hand when you go for that first job interview,
so here are a few tips ...

CHOOSE RELEVANT COURSES

If your school does a First Aid course, then take it, because
first aid is a prerequisite for many jobs in this area. Doing a
course such as an Entry Level Certificate in Skills for
Working Life (Health and Social Care), or a BTEC Level 1
Introductory Certificate or a Diploma in Health and Social
Care, will show employers that you have a real interest in this
area. If you think you might like to teach English as a foreign

language (TEFL), take modern language GCSEs and A levels to show you have linguistic flair. Joining a local or school sports team or sports club is great experience for those who want to go into the health and fitness sector.

GET SOME RELEVANT EXPERIENCE

Help at your local youth club, become a Young Leader with the Scouts or the Girl Guides (see page 14), help out at a children's summer camp over the summer holidays and do whatever you can to get some hands-on experience. It is also a good idea to take the Duke of Edinburgh's award as it will show that you have real potential and good leadership skills, as well as giving you the opportunity to get involved in your local community. If nothing else, babysit!

What are you waiting for? Get out there and start making a difference!

GET OUT AND MEET PEOPLE

Working in this sector is all about meeting a constantly changing flow of people, so hone your social skills by getting out and talking to as many different people from as many different cultural and social backgrounds and age groups as possible. Getting a Saturday job in a shop is a great way of meeting new people.

Although Britain has an ageing population there will always be a need for people to work with children and teenagers, so this is an area where, once qualified, it will never be difficult for you to find employment. As there are youth services all over the country you should be able to find work wherever you eventually decide to live, although you should be aware that the exact balance of jobs on offer varies in different areas of the country.

Working with young people may not be the most financially rewarding career but the personal rewards in terms of job satisfaction and fulfilment can be huge. Remember, not everyone is suited to this work – but if you are, your skills and commitment are not only sorely needed but they will also be hugely appreciated. So what are you waiting for? Get out there and start making a difference!

Here's a final checklist that will help you decide if a future working with young people is really for you. Just tick the 'Yes' or 'No' boxes.

THE LAST WORD

✔ TICK YES OR NO

DO YOU LIKE BEING AROUND YOUNG PEOPLE?
- [ ] YES
- [ ] NO

DO YOU HAVE LOTS OF ENERGY?
- [ ] YES
- [ ] NO

ARE YOU A PATIENT PERSON?
- [ ] YES
- [ ] NO

CAN YOU SEE ANOTHER PERSON'S POINT OF VIEW?
- [ ] YES
- [ ] NO

CAN YOU SHOW AUTHORITY WHEN NEEDED?
- [ ] YES
- [ ] NO

ARE YOU ABLE TO COMMUNICATE EFFECTIVELY WITH ALL AGE GROUPS?
- [ ] YES
- [ ] NO

CAN YOU THINK OUTSIDE THE BOX?
- [ ] YES
- [ ] NO

IS MAKING A REAL DIFFERENCE IN SOMEONE ELSE'S LIFE IMPORTANT TO YOU?
- [ ] YES
- [ ] NO

If you answered 'YES' to all these questions, CONGRATULATIONS! WORKING WITH YOUNG PEOPLE IS THE RIGHT CAREER FOR YOU!

If you answered 'NO' to any of the questions, a career more loosely connected to working with young people may suit your skills and strengths better. For example, you could work in administration or in a secretarial position at a school, crèche or playgroup.

Resources

BOOKS

The Directory of Teacher Training Courses (2006, Trotman Publishing)

The Guardian Guide to Careers, ed. Jimmy Leach (2005, Atlantic/Guardian Books)

Teaching Uncovered, Brin Best (2006, Trotman Publishing)

Working with Young People 2004–2005, ed. Clare Horton (2005, Guardian Books)

USEFUL ORGANISATIONS

CACHE (COUNCIL FOR AWARDS IN CHILDREN'S CARE AND EDUCATION)
Tel: 01727 818616
Website: www.cache.org.uk

CACHE develops courses for people who want to work in the childcare sector. In the Qualifications area of its website there is a series of questions that will give you a better idea of which course will suit your skills and needs the most.

CONNEXIONS
Tel: 080 8001 3219
Website: www.connexions.gov.uk and www.connexionscard.com

Connexions is aimed primarily at providing careers advice and guidance to 13- to 19-year-olds, but it is an excellent source of information for all ages. The Career Zone section of the Connexionscard site includes a Career Bank that lists hundreds of careers with job descriptions and details on who to contact for more information.

DEPARTMENT FOR EDUCATION AND SKILLS (DfES)
Website: www.dfes.gov.uk and
www.dfes.gov.uk/childrenswf/qualifications

The Department for Education and Skills has an excellent website giving information on Career Development Loans and other funding. The second of the two websites listed above will take you to the Children's Workforce Qualifications area where you can check whether the course you wish to take leads to a recognised qualification.

EDEXCEL
Tel: 0870 240 9800
Website: www.edexcel.org.uk

Edexcel is responsible for BTEC qualifications including First Diplomas, National Diplomas and Higher National Certificates and Diplomas (HNCs and HNDs). Go to the Health and Social Care section of their website for an overview of qualifications in this area, from the Entry Level Certificate in Skills for Working Life (Health and Social Care), to the BTEC Diploma in Specialised Play for Sick Children and Young People.

GSCC (GENERAL SOCIAL CARE COUNCIL)
Tel: 020 7397 5800
Website: www.gscc.org.uk

The General Social Care Council registers social care workers and regulates their conduct. Their website explains how you can become registered, explains codes of practice and also has information on social work courses and bursaries.

LEARN DIRECT
Tel: 0800 100 900
Website: www.learndirect-advice.co.uk

This free helpline and website can give you impartial advice and information about learning and courses available across the country. Just enter a subject keyword (such as 'childcare') and the area of the country where you wish to study, and a list of the relevant courses will be displayed.

LG JOBS
Website: www.lgjobs.com

If you are looking for a position with your local council, this local government official recruitment website can really help. Not only does it tell you what jobs are available, it also gives detailed job descriptions including qualifications necessary and salary range.

NATIONAL CHILDMINDING ASSOCIATION
Website: www.ncma.org.uk

The National Childminding Association promotes the sector and aims to support those working within it. It now has 50,000 members. It organises courses of training, and provides information to those interested in working in the sector. Its website also contains information on the government's voluntary Childcare Approval Scheme.

NYA (NATIONAL YOUTH AGENCY)
Website: www.nya.org.uk

The NYA aims to support and advance those involved in youth work. It helps shape youth policy and works to improve youth services. Its website offers comprehensive information on qualifications and training and also contains details of job vacancies at the NYA itself.

SOCIAL WORK RECRUITMENT CAMPAIGN SITE
Website: www.socialworkcareers.co.uk

Set up by the Department of Health, this website is about careers for those with or without a degree qualification. It allows you to discover what social work is all about, which universities do which courses and whether you are eligible for a bursary, and to view social work vacancies at various local authorities.

SURE START
Website: www.childcarecareers.gov.uk and www.childcarelink.gov.uk

The current government has developed the Sure Start programme to upgrade early years provision and to offer supportive training to those who wish to work in this sector. This excellent website gives really in-depth information about working in childcare. Find out what jobs are available, which you would be most suitable for and what's in it for you.

TEACHERNET
Website: www.teachernet.gov.uk

Developed by the DfES, TeacherNet offers support to the education profession. On the website you can find out about courses, learn about new developments in education, read news stories and even download publications.

TRAINING AND DEVELOPMENT AGENCY FOR SCHOOLS
Tel: 0845 6000 991
Website: www.teach.gov.uk

Useful if you are thinking about teaching as a career, this website gives detailed information about the profession including different career paths and the possibilities of promotion.

YJB (YOUTH JUSTICE BOARD)
Tel: 020 7271 3033
Website: www.youth-justice-board.gov.uk

The YJB oversees the youth justice system in both England and Wales. It works in the courts and also with young offenders who are on bail, to prevent them from reoffending. You can find out how to become a professional or a volunteer at the Getting Involved section of the website.

VOLUNTARY ORGANISATIONS

DO-IT
Website: www.do-it.org.uk

This website is part of the YouthNet charity and it is the only national database of volunteering opportunities in the UK.

THE DUKE OF EDINBURGH'S AWARD SCHEME
Website: www.theaward.org

The official website for the Duke of Edinburgh's Award Scheme contains in-depth information on what the award is all about.

THE GIRL GUIDES
Website: www.girlguiding.org.uk

If you would like to find out more about becoming a Young Leader or a Unit Leader with the Girl Guides there is specific information on this website.

THE SCOUTS
Website: www.scouts.org.uk

If you would like to find out more about becoming a Young Leader or a Unit Leader with the Scouts there is specific information on this website.